MACBETH

MACBETH

By William Shakespeare

Adapted by Diana Stewart
Illustrated by Charles Shaw

Raintree Publishers
Milwaukee • Toronto • Melbourne • London

Library of Congress Number: 81-19273

1 2 3 4 5 6 7 8 9 0 84 83 82

Printed and bound in the United States of America.

Library of Congress Cataloging in Publication Data

Stewart, Diana.
   Macbeth

   Summary: An adaptation of the tragedy of
prophecy and royal murder set in medieval
Scotland.
   [1. Scotland—History—To 1057—Drama.
2. Plays] I. Shaw, Charles, 1941-   ill.
II. Shakespeare, William, 1564-1616. Macbeth.
III. Title.
PR2823.A25 1982   812'.54   81-19273
ISBN 0-8172-1681-2   AACR2

CAST OF CHARACTERS

Duncan — King of Scotland
Malcolm — Duncan's son
Donalbain — Duncan's son

Generals of the King's army:
Macbeth — Thane of Glamis
Banquo

Noblemen of Scotland:
Macduff — Thane of Fife
Lennox
Ross
Angus

Siward — Earl of Northumberland,
general of the English forces
Young Siward — his son
Seyton — an officer attending on Macbeth
A Porter
A Doctor

Lady Macbeth
Gentlewoman — attending on Lady Macbeth

The Weird Sisters — three witches

Various apparitions, lords, gentlemen, officers, soldiers,
murderers, attendants, and messengers

THE SETTING
The setting for the play is Scotland in about 1050 A.D.,
and England at the palace of Edward, King of England.
At this time Scotland is divided into different sections.
Each is ruled over by a thane — or lord. Duncan, King of
Scotland, rules over all.

ACT I

Scene 1

During the day a battle has been raging against the enemies of Duncan, King of Scotland. Macbeth — Thane of Glamis and also a general in the King's army — has led his soldiers to victory.

The scene is a heath — a wild, open place — not far from the battlefield. The three witches enter as a drum sounds. The lightning and thunder continue.

THIRD WITCH. A drum, a drum!
Macbeth doth come!

(Macbeth enters with Banquo — a nobleman of Scotland and also a general in the army.)

MACBETH. So foul and fair a day I have not seen.

(Banquo sees the three witches.)

BANQUO. What are these, so withered and wild,
That do not look like the people of the earth,
And yet are on it? (To the witches) You should
be women,
And yet your beards forbid me to think
That you are so.

MACBETH. Speak, if you can. What are you?

FIRST WITCH. All hail, Macbeth! Hail to thee, Thane
of Glamis!

SECOND WITCH. All hail, Macbeth! Hail to thee, Thane
of Cawdor!

THIRD WITCH. All hail, Macbeth, that shalt be king hereafter!

(The witches now turn to speak to Banquo.)

WITCHES. Hail!

FIRST WITCH. Lesser than Macbeth, and greater.

SECOND WITCH. Not so happy, yet much happier.

THIRD WITCH. Thou shalt be the father of kings,
Though thou be none.
So all hail, Macbeth and Banquo!

FIRST WITCH. Banquo and Macbeth, all hail!

MACBETH. (To the witches) Tell me more!
I know I am Thane of Glamis,
But how of Cawdor? The Thane of Cawdor lives,
And to be king, I cannot believe,
No more than to be Cawdor. Say from where
You owe this strange news.

(The witches vanish.)

BANQUO. Where are they vanished?

MACBETH. Into the air. I wish they had stayed!

BANQUO. Were they here? Or are we mad?

MACBETH. Your children shall be kings.

BANQUO. You shall be king!

MACBETH. And Thane of Cawdor too. Went it not so?

(Ross and Angus — two of King Duncan's noblemen —
enter.)

ROSS. Macbeth, the king hath happily received
The news of thy success.

ANGUS. We are sent to give thee thanks
From our royal master.

ROSS. And he bade me call thee Thane of Cawdor.
Hail, most worthy thane!

BANQUO. What, can the devil speak true?

MACBETH. The Thane of Cawdor lives. Why do you
dress me
In borrowed robes?

ANGUS. He who was the thane still lives,
But treason — confessed and proved —
Has overthrown him.

7

MACBETH. (To himself) Glamis, and Thane of Cawdor —
And the greatest is yet to come!
(To Ross and Angus)
I thank you, gentlemen. (To Banquo)
Do you not hope your children shall be kings?
Those that gave the Thane of Cawdor to me
Promised no less to them.

BANQUO. It is strange. But sometimes the powers
of darkness
Tell us truths to win our souls.

MACBETH. Think upon what has happened.
We will speak of it together again.

(They exit.)

Scene 2

The scene is Macbeth's castle at Inverness. Lady Macbeth enters reading a letter she has just received from her husband.

LADY MACBETH. "The hags met me on the day of our victory, and I have learned that they have more than human knowledge. When I burned in desire to question them further, they made themselves air and vanished. While I stood stunned by the wonder of it, messengers came from the king. They called me 'Thane of Cawdor' just as those Weird Sisters had said. This news have I thought good to tell thee, my dearest wife. Rejoice with me and put it in thy heart. Farewell."

(Lady Macbeth speaks now to herself.)

Glamis thou art, and now Cawdor, and shalt be king!
Yet, Macbeth, I am afraid of thy nature.
It is too full of the milk of human kindness
To catch the chance. Thou wouldst be great. Thou
Art not without ambition, but without
The ruthlessness that must attend it.
Come home, Macbeth, that I may give thee courage

And drive from thy mind all that keeps
Thee from being king!

(A messenger enters.)

LADY MACBETH. What is your news?

MESSENGER. The king comes here tonight.

LADY MACBETH. Thou art mad to say it!

MESSENGER. It is true. Macbeth, our thane, is also coming.

LADY MACBETH. This is great news!

(The messenger exits. An evil plan forms in Lady Macbeth's mind. She plans to kill the king so that Macbeth can inherit the crown. Macbeth enters.)

LADY MACBETH. Great Glamis! Worthy Cawdor!
And greater yet to be!

MACBETH. My dearest love,
Duncan comes here tonight.

LADY MACBETH. And when does he leave?

MACBETH. Tomorrow.

LADY MACBETH. Oh, never shall he see the morning sun!
Provide for the king,
And put the rest into my hands.

(Macbeth understands what his wife means, and he is frightened.)

MACBETH. We will speak further.

LADY MACBETH. Only appear untroubled,
And leave the rest to me!

(They exit.)

Scene 3

King Duncan has arrived at the castle. Lady Macbeth has told Macbeth of her plan. They will murder the king during the night. Macbeth leaves the banquet hall where the king is eating. He is ambitious. He wants to be king, but he is afraid of committing the crime — and of being caught! He argues with himself.

MACBETH. If it were done when 'tis done, then 'twere well
    It were done quickly!

(Lady Macbeth enters.)

    How now! What news?

LADY MACBETH. He has supped. Why have you left
    the chamber?

MACBETH. We will proceed no further in this business!

LADY MACBETH. Are you afraid?
    Would you live a coward?

MACBETH. Prithee, peace!
    I dare do all that may become a man.
    Who dares do more is none!

(Lady Macbeth is disgusted with her husband. He has promised her his help, and now he is afraid.)

LADY MACBETH. When you dared to do it, then you
    were a man!
    I have given suck to my children, and know
    How tender it is to love the babe that milks me.
    I would, while it was smiling in my face,
    Have plucked my nipple from his boneless gums,
    And dashed the brains out, if I had broken my
    Word as you have done!

MACBETH. If we should fail?

LADY MACBETH. We fail!
    But screw your courage to the sticking place,
    And we'll not fail. When Duncan is asleep
    I will ply his servants with wine until
    They sleep as though in a death.
    Then what cannot you and I perform upon
    The unguarded Duncan? We will then put upon
    His sleeping guards the guilt of our murder.

MACBETH. When we have used their very daggers,
    And marked them with blood,

All will believe they have done the deed!

LADY MACBETH. Who would dare believe it other?

MACBETH. So be it! I am settled!
Away, and mock the time with fairest show.
False face must hide what the false heart doth know.

(They exit.)

ACT II

Scene 1

The scene is Macbeth's castle after midnight. Banquo meets Macbeth in the courtyard.

BANQUO. What, sire, not yet at rest? The king is a-bed.
He hath been in unusual pleasure, and
Sent forth gifts to you. He greets your wife with
this diamond
And the name of most kind hostess.

MACBETH. I give him thanks.

BANQUO. I dreamt last night of the three Weird Sisters.
To you they have showed some truth.

MACBETH. I think not of them.
Yet, when we can find an hour
We would spend it in some words upon that business,
If you would grant the time.

BANQUO. At your kindest leisure.

(Banquo exits.)

(Macbeth is left alone. The hour has come for him to murder Duncan, and he sees an apparition — a ghostly vision — of a dagger.)

MACBETH. Is this a dagger which I see before me,
The handle toward my hand? Come, let me
clutch thee!

(He reaches out for it, but there is nothing there.)

I have thee not, and yet I see thee still. Art thou but
A dagger of the mind, a false creation,
Proceeding from the fevered brain?

*(The dagger leads him on toward the king's chamber. A
bell rings.)*

I go, and it is done. The bell invites me.
Hear it not, Duncan, for it is a sound
That summons thee to heaven, or to hell!

(He exits.)

Scene 2

The scene is the same a short time later. Lady Macbeth
enters. She has already given the king's guards the
drugged wine and seen them fall asleep.

LADY MACBETH. That which hath made them drunk hath
    made me bold!
What hath quenched them hath given me fire.

MACBETH. *(Calling from within the king's chamber.)*
    Who's there? What, ho!

LADY MACBETH. Alack, I am afraid they have awaked
    And it is not done! The attempt and not the deed
Destroys us. Hark! I laid their daggers ready.
He could not miss them. Had the king not resembled
My father as he slept, I would have done it!

(Macbeth enters.)

LADY MACBETH. My husband!

MACBETH. I have done the deed. Didst thou not hear
    a noise?

LADY MACBETH. I heard the owl scream and the crickets cry.
    Did you not speak?

MACBETH. As I came?

LADY MACBETH. Ay.

MACBETH. Hark!
Who sleeps in the second chamber?

LADY MACBETH. Donalbain, the king's son.

(Macbeth looks at his blood-covered hands.)

MACBETH. This is a sorry sight.

LADY MACBETH. A foolish thought, to say a sorry sight.

MACBETH. One servant did laugh in his sleep,
And one cried "Murder!"
They did wake each other. I stood and heard them.
They did say their prayers,
One cried "God bless us!" and "Amen" the other.
I could not say "Amen,"
When they did say "God bless us!"

LADY MACBETH. Consider it not so deeply!

MACBETH. But why could I not say "Amen?"
I had most need of blessing, and "Amen"
Stuck in my throat.

LADY MACBETH. Speak not of these things. It will make
us mad!

MACBETH. Methought I heard a voice cry "Sleep no more!
Macbeth does murder sleep."

LADY MACBETH. Think not such harmful thoughts!
Go get some water,
And wash this blood from your hands.

(She sees that Macbeth still has the guards' daggers.)

Why did you bring these daggers from the chamber?
They must lie there. Go carry them, and smear
The sleeping servants with blood.

MACBETH. I'll go no more!
I am afraid to think what I have done.
I dare not look on it again!

LADY MACBETH. Give me the daggers! Weak of purpose!
I'll smear the faces of the guards with blood,
For it must seem their guilt.

17

(Lady Macbeth exits. Macbeth hears the sound of knocking.)

MACBETH. Where is that knocking?
 What is wrong with me when every noise appalls me?
 What a bloody hand is here!
 Will all the ocean wash this blood
 Clean from my hand? No! My hand will instead
 Stain the great seas and make them red.

(Lady Macbeth returns.)

LADY MACBETH. My hands are now of your color,
 But I would be ashamed to wear a heart so cowardly.

(The sound of knocking is heard again.)

LADY MACBETH. I hear a knocking at the south entry.
 We must retire to our chamber.
 A little water clears us of this deed.
 How easy it is then!

(More knocking sounds.)

LADY MACBETH. Hark! More knocking.
 Get on your nightgown, lest we be found awake.
 Be not so cowardly in your thoughts!

(The knocking continues.)

MACBETH. Wake Duncan with thy knocking!
 I would thou couldst!

(They exit.)

Scene 3

The scene is in the castle. A Porter enters to answer the knocking at the door.

PORTER. Here's a knocking indeed!
 Knock, knock, knock!
 Who in the devil's name is there?

(He opens the door and Macduff, Thane of Fife, and Lennox, a nobleman of Scotland, enter.)

MACDUFF. Enough, old man! Is thy master stirring?

(Macbeth enters.)

Our knocking has awakened him. Here he comes.

LENNOX. Good morrow, noble sir.

MACBETH. Good morrow, both.

MACDUFF. Is the king stirring, worthy thane?

MACBETH. Not yet.

MACDUFF. He did command me to call on him early.
I have almost missed the hour.

MACBETH. I'll bring you to him. This is the door.

(Macbeth stands aside to let Macduff pass. Macduff exits into the king's chamber.)

LENNOX. The night has been strange. Where we slept
Our chimneys were blown down.
Crying was heard in the air — strange screams
of death
And prophesying with terrible voices
Of trouble and confused events.
Some say, the earth
Was feverous and did shake.

(Macduff re-enters.)

MACDUFF. O horror, horror, horror! My tongue and heart
Cannot believe or name such horror!

MACBETH AND LENNOX. What's the matter?

MACDUFF. Death now hath made his masterpiece!

MACBETH. What is it you say? Whose death?

LENNOX. Mean you His Majesty?

MACDUFF. Approach the chamber, and blind your sight
With the horror of it! Do not bid me speak!
See, and then speak yourselves.

(Macbeth and Lennox exit into the king's chamber. Macduff calls out the alarm.)

MACDUFF. Awake! Awake!

Ring the alarm-bell. Murder and treason!
Banquo and Donalbain! Malcolm! Awake!
And look on death itself! Up, up, and see!
Malcolm! Banquo!
As from your graves rise up, and walk like spirits
To see this horror. Ring the bell!

(The bell rings the alarm. Banquo enters.)

MACDUFF. O Banquo, Banquo!
Our royal master's murdered.

BANQUO. Dear Duff, I prithee, say it is not so.

(Macbeth and Lennox re-enter with Ross.)

MACBETH. Had I but died an hour before this time!
From this instant there's nothing left in life!
Fame, grace and goodness is dead.
The wine of life is drawn, and the mere dregs
Are left this earth.

(King Duncan's sons — Malcolm and Donalbain — enter.)

DONALBAIN. What is amiss?

MACBETH. You are, and do not know it.
The spring, the head, the fountain of your blood
Is stopped. The very source of it is stopped.

MACDUFF. Your royal father is murdered.

MALCOLM. O! By whom?

LENNOX. Those servants of his chamber, it seems, had
done it.
Their hands and faces were all smeared with blood.
So were their daggers, which unwiped we found
Upon their pillows.
They stared, and were fearful. No man's life
Was to be trusted with them.

MACBETH. O, yet I do repent me of my fury,
That I did kill them.

MACDUFF. Why did you so?

MACBETH. Who can be wise when furious,

Loyal and calm in such a moment? No man.
My violent love outran my reason.

BANQUO. When we have overcome this present grief,
Let us meet and question this most bloody piece
of work.
I would fight this treason and malice.

MACDUFF. And I!

ALL. So all.

MACBETH. Let us meet together in the hall.

ACT III
Scene 1

The scene is Forres, in the palace where Macbeth now
rules as king. Banquo enters and speaks to himself. He is
suspicious of Macbeth.

BANQUO. Thou has it now, Macbeth — King, Cawdor,
Glamis, all.
Just as the weird women promised, and I fear what
Thou didst for it. Yet it was said
That myself should be the father of many kings.
But hush, no more.

(*Trumpets sound announcing the entrance of Macbeth as
King, Lady Macbeth as Queen, Lennox, Ross, and various
lords, ladies, and attendants.*)

MACBETH. Here is our chief guest, Banquo.
Sir, tonight we hold a state supper,
And I'll request your presence.

BANQUO. Let it be as Your Highness commands.

MACBETH. Do you ride this afternoon?

BANQUO. Ay, my good lord.

MACBETH. Fail not to attend our feast.

BANQUO. My lord, I will not.

MACBETH. We hear that our bloody cousins, Malcolm
and Donalbain,
Are in England and Ireland. They do not confess
Their cruel murder and are said to be telling
strange tales.
But we will speak of that tomorrow.
Does your son Fleance go riding with you?

BANQUO. Ay, my good lord.

MACBETH. Then farewell till you return tonight.

(Everyone exits but Macbeth.)

MACBETH. To be king is nothing.
I would be safely king. I fear Banquo.
He dares much,
And he hath a wisdom that doth guide his courage.
There is none but he whose being I do fear.

The Weird Sisters put the name of king upon me,
But they hailed him father to a line of kings.
Upon my head they placed a barren crown,
No son of mine to rule after me.

If it be so, for Banquo's sons have I
Murdered the gracious Duncan,
To make them kings!
Rather than that: Come, Fate, to the battle!
And aid me to the death!

*(A servant enters with the two men Macbeth is waiting
for. They are two murderers he has hired to kill Banquo
and his son Fleance. The servant exits, leaving the three
men alone.)*

MACBETH. Both of you know that Banquo is my enemy.
Every minute he lives it is a threat against my life.

FIRST MURDERER. My lord, we shall
Do what you command of us.

MACBETH. The time has come. The deed must be
done tonight.

And somewhere away from the palace.
Fleance, his son, keeps him company.
His death is no less important to me
Than his father's.

BOTH MURDERERS. Just as you say, my lord.

(The two murderers exit, leaving Macbeth alone.)

MACBETH. It is finished. Banquo, thy soul's flight,
If it find heaven, must find it tonight.

(He exits.)

Scene 2

A banquet has been prepared in one of the great halls of the palace. Macbeth and Lady Macbeth enter. With them are various lords of the court and servants.

As the party seats themselves around the table, Macbeth sees one of the murderers standing at the door. He goes to him.

MACBETH. There's blood upon thy face.

MURDERER. 'Tis Banquo's then.

MACBETH. Is he dead?

MURDERER. My lord, his throat is cut. That I did for him.

MACBETH. Thou art the best of the cut-throats.
Didst thou do the same for Fleance, his son?

MURDERER. Most royal sir, Fleance is escaped.

MACBETH. (To himself) Then comes my fit again.
I have such doubts and fears!
(To the murderer) But Banquo's dead?

MURDERER. Ay, my good lord. Dead in a ditch he bides,
With twenty gashes on his head.

MACBETH. Thanks for that. Now, get thee gone.

(The murderer exits. But just as Macbeth is about to take his place at the table, the ghost of Banquo enters. The ghost sits in Macbeth's place. No one else can see him but Macbeth.)

LENNOX. May it please Your Highness sit
    And grace us with your royal company.

MACBETH. The table's full.

LENNOX. Here is a place reserved, sir.

MACBETH. Where?

LENNOX. Here, my good lord. What is it that troubles
    Your Highness?

MACBETH. Which of you have done this?

LORDS. What, my good lord?

(Macbeth looks at the ghost in horror.)

MACBETH. Thou canst not say I did it. Never shake
    Thy gory locks at me!

ROSS. Gentlemen, rise, His Highness is not well.

LADY MACBETH. (She is concerned about her husband, but she
    doesn't want the others to know.)
    Sit, worthy friends. My lord is often thus,
    And hath been from his youth. Pray you, keep
        your seats.
    The fit is momentary. He will soon be well again.
    If you make much of it, you shall offend him.
    Feed, and regard him not.

(She speaks angrily to Macbeth.)

Are you a man?

(Macbeth points to the place where the ghost sits.)

MACBETH. Prithee, see there! Behold! Look! Lo, how
    say you?
    Our graves send those that we bury back!

(The ghost vanishes.)

LADY MACBETH. Are you mad?

MACBETH. I saw him — Banquo!

LADY MACBETH. (Not believing him.) Fie, for shame!

MACBETH. Blood hath been shed before now.

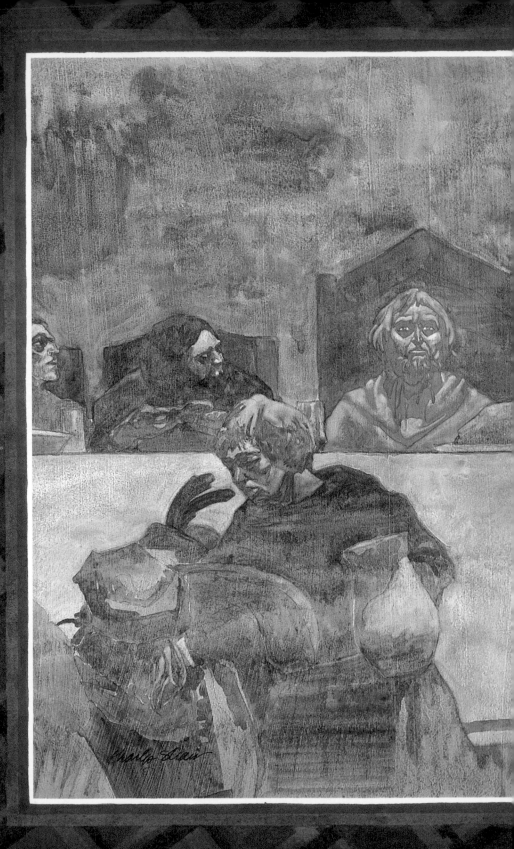

Murders have been performed
Too terrible for the ear. The time has been
That, when the brains were out, the man would die,
And there an end. But now they rise again.

(Lady Macbeth is getting more and more worried. Macbeth is betraying himself, and all the noblemen can hear.)

LADY MACBETH. My worthy lord, your noble friends
    look on!

MACBETH. I do forget.

(He turns to the guests at the banquet.)

My most worthy friends,
I have a strange illness which is nothing
To those that know me. Come, love and health to all.
Then I'll sit down. Give me some wine — fill full!

(The ghost of Banquo re-enters and stands behind Macbeth.)

MACBETH. I drink to the general joy of the whole table,
    And to our dear friend Banquo, whom we miss.
    Would he were here! To all and him we drink!

(Suddenly, the ghost moves and Macbeth alone sees him.)

MACBETH. Away! And quit my sight! Let the earth
    hide thee!
    Thy blood is cold. Thou has no sight in those eyes
    Which glare at me!

LADY MACBETH. *(Frightened now that Macbeth will betray them.)*
    Think of this, good friends, as a common thing.
    'Tis nothing else, only it spoils our pleasure.

(Again the ghost vanishes.)

MACBETH. Ah, such a sight!

ROSS. What sight, my lord!

LADY MACBETH. (Quickly, before Macbeth can answer)
    I pray you, speak not, sir. He grows worse and worse.
    Questions enrage him. At once, good night.

(All the lords rise and prepare to leave at once.)

LENNOX. Good night, and better health
    Attend His Majesty!

LADY MACBETH. A kind good night to all!

(They all exit except Macbeth and Lady Macbeth.)

MACBETH. It will have blood. They say blood will
        have blood.
    Stones have been known to move and trees to speak!
    Where was Macduff?

LADY MACBETH. Did you send for him, sir?

MACBETH. Ay, I would know why he does not come at
        my command!
    Tomorrow I will seek out the Weird Sisters.
    More shall they speak. For now I am determined
        to know!

(They exit.)

ACT IV

Scene 1

The witches are gathered together in a cave. In the middle is a boiling caldron around which they stand. Thunder sounds in the distance.

FIRST WITCH. Thrice the stripéd cat hath mewed.

SECOND WITCH. Thrice and once the hedge-pig whines.

THIRD WITCH. Demons cry — "'Tis time, 'tis time."

FIRST WITCH. Round about the caldron go;
    In the poisoned entrails throw.
    Toad, that under cold stone
    Days and nights has thirty-one,
    Sweltered venom sleeping got,
    Boil thou first in the charmed pot.

ALL. Double, double toil and trouble;
    Fire burn and caldron bubble.

SECOND WITCH. Fillet of a fenny snake
    In the caldron boil and bake;
    Eye of newt and toe of frog,
    Wool of bat and tongue of dog,
    Adder's fork and blindworm's sting,
    Lizard's leg and howlet's wing,
    For a charm of powerful trouble
    Like a hell-broth boil and bubble.

ALL. Double, double toil and trouble;
    Fire burn and caldron bubble.

THIRD WITCH. Cool it with a baboon's blood,
    Then the charm is firm and good.

FIRST WITCH. By the pricking of my thumbs,
    Something wicked this way comes.
    Open, locks,
    Whoever knocks!

(Macbeth enters.)

MACBETH. How now, you secret, black, and midnight hags!
    What is it you do?

ALL. A deed without a name.

MACBETH. I command you! Answer me what I ask of you.

FIRST WITCH. Say, if you would rather hear it from
      our mouths
    Or from our masters.

MACBETH. Call your masters. Let me see them!

*(The First Witch pours some blood into the caldron. A clap of
thunder is heard. The first apparition rises from the caldron.
It is just a head.)*

MACBETH. Tell me thou unknown power —

FIRST WITCH. He knows thy thought.
    Hear his speech, but say thou nought.

FIRST APPARITION. Macbeth! Macbeth! Macbeth!
    Beware Macduff.

Beware the Thane of Fife. Dismiss me, enough.

(The head disappears back into the caldron.)

MACBETH. Whatever thou art, for thy good
    caution — thanks!
Thou hast guessed my fear aright. But one
    word more —

FIRST WITCH. He will not be commanded. Here's another,
    More potent than the first.

(There is a second clap of thunder and the second apparition appears. It is a bloody child.)

SECOND APPARITION. Be bloody, bold and resolute. Laugh
    to scorn
The power of man. For none of woman born
Shall harm Macbeth.

(The second apparition disappears.)

MACBETH. Then live, Macduff. What need I fear of thee?
    But yet, I'll make double sure. Thou shalt not live!

(The third clap of thunder brings the third apparition. It is a child wearing a crown and carrying a tree in his hand.)

THIRD APPARITION. Be lion-mettled, proud, and take no care
    Who chafes, who frets, or where conspirers are.
Macbeth shall never vanquished be until
Great Birnam Wood to high Dunsinane Hill
Shall come against him.

(The third apparition disappears back into the caldron.)

MACBETH. That will never be!
    Who can move the forest, bid the tree
Unfix his earth-bound roots?
Sweet words — good! Yet my heart
Throbs to know one thing. Tell me, if your art
Can tell so much — shall Banquo's son ever
Reign in this kingdom?

ALL. Seek to know no more.

MACBETH. I will be satisfied. Deny me this,
    And an eternal curse fall on you! Let me know.

(A noise is heard from the caldron.)

MACBETH. What noise is this?

*(The final apparition appears. In a row stand eight kings.
The last is holding a looking glass in his hand. Banquo's
ghost follows them.)*

MACBETH. Thou art the spirit of Banquo! Down!
Thy crown does burn my eye-balls.
(To the witches)
Filthy hags! Why do you show me this? A fourth?
What, will the line stretch out to the crack of doom?
Another yet! A seventh! I'll see no more.
And yet the eighth appears, who bears a mirror
Which shows me many more.
Horrible sight! Now I see 'tis true.
Dead Banquo smiles upon me,
And points at them for his. What, is this so?

FIRST WITCH. Ay, sir, all this is so. But why
Stands Macbeth thus amazed?
Come, sisters, cheer we up his sprites,
And show the best of our delights.

(Music sounds. The witches dance and then vanish.)

MACBETH. Where are they? Gone? Lennox!

*(Lennox enters from outside the cave where he has been
waiting.)*

LENNOX. What is Your Grace's will?

MACBETH. Saw you the Weird Sisters?

LENNOX. No, my lord.

MACBETH. Came they not by you?

LENNOX. No indeed, my lord.

MACBETH. I did hear the galloping of horse.
Who was it came by?

LENNOX. 'Tis two or three, my lord, that brings you word
Macduff is fled to England.

(Macbeth knows now that Macduff is his enemy. He will seek revenge on Macduff.)

MACBETH. (To himself) The castle of Macduff I will surprise.
Seize upon Fife, give to the edge of the sword
His wife, his babes, and all unfortunate souls
That follow him in his line. No boasting like a fool;
This deed I'll do before this purpose cool!

(They exit.)

Scene 2

The scene is in England at the palace of King Edward. Macduff has come to find Malcolm and convince him that they must join together to fight against Macbeth. Enter Macduff and Malcolm.

MACDUFF. Not in all of horrid hell
Can come a devil more cursed
In evils to top Macbeth.

MALCOLM. Devilish Macbeth! Macduff, what I am
Is thine and my poor country's to command.
Indeed, Old Siward — Earl of Northumberland
And general of the English forces — stands ready,
With ten thousand warlike men already armed.
They set forth for Scotland. Now we'll
Together go!

(Ross — Macduff's cousin — enters.)

MACDUFF. See who comes here! My ever gentle cousin.
Welcome hither.

ROSS. Sir, amen.

MACDUFF. Stand Scotland where it did?

ROSS. Alas, poor country!
Sighs and groans and shrieks rend the air.
Violent sorrow dwells in the hearts of
Our countrymen. Scotland cannot
Be called our mother, but our grave!

MALCOLM. What's the newest grief?

ROSS. Each minute brings forth a new one.

MACDUFF. How does my wife and all my children?

ROSS. Let not your ears despise my tongue forever
      When I speak the most horrible words
      That ever yet they heard.

MACDUFF. Humh! I guess at it! Speak!

ROSS. Your castle was surprised. Your wife and babes
      Savagely slaughtered.

MALCOLM. Merciful heaven!

MACDUFF. My children too?

ROSS. Wife, children, servants, all
      That could be found.

MACDUFF. My wife killed too?

ROSS. I have said.

      *(Macduff is almost too stunned to take in the news. Grief
      holds him speechless.)*

MALCOLM. Macduff, be comforted.
      Let's make us our great revenge
      To cure this deadly grief.

MACDUFF. All my pretty ones?
      Did you say all? O hell-kite! All?
      What, all my pretty chickens and their mother
      At one fell swoop?

MALCOLM. Take it like a man.

MACDUFF. I shall do so.
      But I must also feel it as a man.
      I cannot but remember such things
      That were most precious to me. Did heaven look on
      And would not take their part? Sinful Macduff!
      They were all struck for thee! Worthless that I am,
      Not for their own faults, but for mine
      Fell slaughter on their souls. Heaven rest them now!

MALCOLM. Let grief change to anger!
    Dull not the heart — enrage it!

MACDUFF. Ay! Without delay! Face to face
    Bring thou Macbeth — this fiend of Scotland —
        and myself.
    Within my sword's length set him. If he escape,
    Heaven forgive him too!

(They exit.)

ACT V

Scene 1

Macbeth and Lady Macbeth have gone to their castle at Dunsinane. He has surrounded the castle with his soldiers. Word has come to him that his enemies in Scotland have joined with the armies of England to defeat him. Lady Macbeth is not well. The deeds she and Macbeth have done are beginning to drive her mad. She is now walking and talking in her sleep. Her servant and the doctor are now watching for her to appear in the room outside her chamber.

DOCTOR. When was it she last walked?

GENTLEWOMAN. Since his Majesty went into the battlefield, I have seen her rise from her bed, throw her nightgown upon her, unlock the chest, take forth paper, fold it, write upon it, afterwards seal it, and again return to bed. Yet she does all this while in a most fast sleep.

(Lady Macbeth enters. She is dressed in her nightgown and carries a lighted candle.)

GENTLEWOMAN. Lo you, here she comes! Fast sleep! Observe her. Stand close.

DOCTOR. You see, her eyes are open.

GENTLEWOMAN. Ah, but they see not.

38

DOCTOR. What is it she does now? Look, how she rubs her hands.

GENTLEWOMAN. It is her habit. She seems to be washing her hands. I have known her continue in this a quarter of an hour.

(Lady Macbeth continues to rub her hands together. She is still sleepwalking and does not know she is being watched.)

LADY MACBETH. Yet here's a spot! Out, damned spot! Out, I say! One, two — why, then 'tis time to do it. Hell is murky!

(She speaks to Macbeth as though he were there.)

Fie, my lord, fie! A soldier and afraid? What need we fear who knows it, when none can call our power to account? Yet who would have thought the old man to have so much blood in him?

DOCTOR. Do you hear that?

LADY MACBETH. The Thane of Fife had a wife. Where is she now?

(She continues to rub her hands, trying to wash off the blood she believes is still on them.)

What, will these hands never be clean?

(Again she speaks to Macbeth.)

No more of that, my lord. No more of that! You ruin all with this starting.

GENTLEWOMAN. She has spoke what she should not. I am sure of that. Heaven knows what she has done.

LADY MACBETH. *(Still rubbing her hands.)*
Here's the smell of the blood still. All the perfumes of Arabia will not sweeten this little hand. Oh, oh, oh!

DOCTOR. What a sigh is there! Her heart is heavy.

GENTLEWOMAN. I would not have such a heart in my bosom for all the world!

LADY MACBETH. *(Speaking again to Macbeth.)*
Wash your hands, put on your nightgown, look not so

pale. I tell you yet again. Banquo's buried. He cannot come out of his grave. To bed, to bed! There's knocking at the gate. Come, come, come, come. Give me your hand. What's done cannot be undone. To bed, to bed, to bed . . . .

(She exits back into her chamber.)

DOCTOR. Unnatural deeds
Do breed unnatural troubles.
God forgive us all! Look after her,
And still keep eyes upon her.
She has astonished my mind and amazed my sight.
I think, but I dare not speak.

GENTLEWOMAN. Goodnight, good doctor.

(They exit.)

Scene 2

Macbeth is inside Dunsinane castle, speaking to the doctor.

MACBETH. Bring me no more bad news.
Till Birnam Wood remove to Dunsinane
I cannot know fear. What's the boy Malcolm?
Was he not born of woman? The spirits that know
All mortal things have told me thus:
"Fear not, Macbeth. No man that's born of woman
Shall ever have power upon thee."

(Macbeth calls for Seyton — the officer who attends him.)

MACBETH. Seyton! (To himself) I am sick at heart —
Seyton, I say! — My way of life is gone!
I have lived long enough. Those things which
I should have in my old age — honor, love,
Obedience, troops of friends — I must not look to
     have.
In their place, curses. — Seyton!

(Seyton enters.)

SEYTON. What's your gracious pleasure?

MACBETH. What news more?

SEYTON. My lord, all is true which was reported.

MACBETH. I'll fight till my flesh is hacked from my bones!
    Give me my armor.

SEYTON. 'Tis not needed yet.

MACBETH. I'll put it on. Send out more horses.
    Search the countryside. Hang those that talk of fear.
    (To the doctor who has been waiting)
    How does your patient, doctor?

DOCTOR. Not so sick, my lord, as she is troubled in mind.

MACBETH. Cure her of that.
    Canst thou not treat a diseased mind
    And pluck out that which weighs upon the heart?

DOCTOR. Therein the patient must treat himself.

MACBETH. Seyton, come. Put mine armor on. Give me
    my staff.
    Doctor, find her disease and cure it to a sound and
    Pure health. Bring me no more ill reports.
    I will not be afraid of death and ruin
    Till Birnam forest come to Dunsinane!

(They exit.)

Scene 3

The English armies have gathered near Birnam Wood.
They have been joined by the Scottish armies that have
turned against Macbeth. Malcolm, Siward, and Macduff
meet with Lennox, Ross, and Angus. They all enter march-
ing with their soldiers.

MALCOLM. Cousins, I hope the days are near at hand
    That Scotland will be safe.

ROSS. We doubt it not.

SIWARD. What wood is this before us?

MACDUFF. The wood of Birnam.

42

MALCOLM. Let every soldier cut him down a branch
And carry it before him. Thereby shall we hide
Our strength and give false report of our numbers.

SOLDIERS. It shall be done.

SIWARD. Then to Dunsinane!

SOLDIERS. To Dunsinane!

Scene 4

Inside Dunsinane castle Macbeth, Seyton, and the soldiers gather with drums and banners.

MACBETH. Hang out our banners on the outward walls!
The cry is still: "They come!" Our castle's strength
Will laugh at an attack. Let our enemies wait outside
The castle walls till hunger and cold eat them up!

(From another part of the castle comes the screaming and crying of women.)

MACBETH. What is that noise?

SEYTON. It is the cry of women, my good lord.

(Seyton exits to find out what the trouble is.)

MACBETH. I have almost forgot the taste of fear.
The time was when my blood would have frozen
To hear a cry like that. But now I have
Supped full with horrors till nothing can make
Me afraid.

(Seyton re-enters.)

SEYTON. The Queen, my lord, is dead!

(Still Macbeth remains calm. He knows now that death is near to them all. Lady Macbeth has taken her own life.)

MACBETH. Tomorrow, and tomorrow, and tomorrow,
Creeps in this petty pace from day to day,
To the last syllable of recorded time;
And all our yesterdays have lighted fools
The way to dusty death.

Out, out, brief candle!
Life's but a walking shadow, a poor player
That struts and frets his hour upon the stage
And then is heard no more. It is a tale
Told by an idiot, full of sound and fury,
Signifying nothing.

(A messenger enters.)

MESSENGER. Gracious my lord, I must report that which
    I saw,
  But I know not how to do it.

MACBETH. Well, say it sir.

MESSENGER. As I did stand my watch upon the hill,
    I looked toward Birnam, and there I thought
    The wood began to move.

MACBETH. Liar and slave!

MESSENGER. Let me endure your wrath if it be not so.
    Within this three miles may you see it coming.
    I say, a moving grove!

MACBETH. If thou speakest false,
    Upon the next tree shalt thou hang!
    If thy speech be truth,
    I care not if thou dost for me the same!

    "Fear not, till Birnam Wood
    Do come to Dunsinane!" the vision said.
    And now a wood comes toward Dunsinane!

    To arms, to arms, and out!
    If this which he says does appear,
    There is no running away nor staying here.
    Ring the alarm bell! Blow, wind! Come, wrack!
    At least we'll die with armor on our back!

(They exit.)

Scene 5

Macbeth enters the battlefield.

MACBETH. They have surrounded me. I cannot flee.
Who is he that was not born of woman?
Such a one am I to fear, or none!

(Siward's son — Young Siward — enters in full armor. His sword is drawn and ready.)

YOUNG SIWARD. What is thy name?

MACBETH. My name's Macbeth.

YOUNG SIWARD. The devil himself could not pronounce a title
More hateful to mine ear.

(They fight, and Macbeth kills Young Siward.)

MACBETH. Thou wast born of woman.
Swords I smile at, weapons laugh and scorn,
That are carried by a man of woman born.

(He exits. Trumpets sound, and Macduff enters looking for Macbeth.)

MACDUFF. Tyrant, show thy face!
My wife and children's ghosts will haunt me still
If thou art slain by any hand but mine!
Let me find him, Fortune! And more I will not ask.

(Macduff sees Macbeth.)

MACDUFF. Turn, hell-hound! Turn!

MACBETH. Get thee back, Macduff! My soul is too heavy
With blood of thine already.

MACDUFF. I have no words.
My voice is in my sword, thou bloodier villain
Than words can give thee!

(Macduff attacks him, and they begin to fight.)

MACBETH. I cannot lose, Macduff!
I bear a charmed life. I cannot be killed
By one born of woman.

MACDUFF. Then despair, Macbeth! And let me
Tell thee: Macduff was from his mother's womb
Untimely ripped.

45

(Macbeth sees now that the witches have tricked him.)

MACBETH. Accursed be the tongue that tells me so!
I'll not fight with thee!

MACDUFF. Then yield thee, coward.

MACBETH. I will not yield
To kiss the ground before young Malcolm's feet
And to be baited and cursed by all of Scotland!

Though Birnam Wood hath come to Dunsinane
And thou hath been born of no woman,
Yet I will fight to the last.

Lay on, Macduff!
And cursed be him that first cries, "Hold, enough!"

(They exit fighting. Alarms and trumpets sound. Malcolm, Siward, Ross and other thanes and soldiers enter.)

MALCOLM. Siward, Macduff is missing, and your noble son.

ROSS. Your son, my lord, has paid a soldier's debt,
But like a man he died.

SIWARD. Why then, he is God's soldier now.
God be with him! Here comes comfort!

(Macduff re-enters. He is carrying Macbeth's bloody head. He bows before Malcolm — now the King of Scotland.)

MACDUFF. Hail, King! For so thou art. Behold
Macbeth's cursed head. The time is free!
Hail, King of Scotland!

(A great flurry of trumpets sounds as the thanes and soldiers celebrate their victory.)

MALCOLM. Noble friends!
This butcher Macbeth and his evil queen are dead!
At the proper time and place
We will give you all your just reward.
So thanks to all, and each of you
We invite to see us crowned at Scone!

(There is a final sound of trumpets, and they exit.)

GLOSSARY

appall   (ə pol´)   to cause shock or dismay

apparition   (ap ə rish´ ən)   a strange or unexpected sight; a ghostly figure

caldron   (kal´ drən)   a large pot or kettle

prophesy   (praf´ ə sē)   a prediction of something that is to come

signify   (sig´ nə fī)   to mean

thane   (thān)   a Scottish lord; one who holds land and is a soldier for the King

untimely   (ən tīm´ lē)   before the proper time; too early

weird   (wird)   magical, strange, or extraordinary